Teach Me...™

English
and
More English

by Judy Mahoney

Teach Me English and More English
Two books in one, twice the fun!
Over 40 songs to sing and learn English

The classic coloring books Teach Me English and Teach Me More English are now combined into a new bind up edition. This new edition includes the original coloring pages from both titles with a 60 minute audio CD. Teach Me English and More English also features eight new pages of expanded vocabulary and activities.

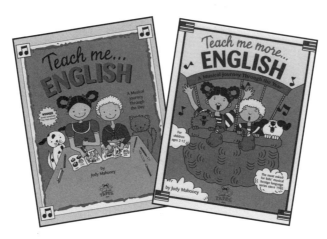

Our mission at Teach Me Tapes is to enrich children through language learning. The **Teach Me...**series of books offers an engaging approach to language acquisition by using familiar children's songs and providing an audio to sing and learn. Studies show that a child's early exposure to new languages and cultures enhances learning skills and promotes a better appreciation of our multicultural world. We believe it is important for children to listen, speak, read and write the language in order to enhance the learning experience. What better gift to offer our youth than the tools and ideas to understand the world we live in?

The English language was developed mainly from the Anglo-Saxon and Norman-French languages. Today, English is the most widely spoken language in the world. In many countries, it is either the native language or a secondary language. Over 350 million people speak English as their native language. It has a very large vocabulary with over 600,000 words, with new words being added every year.

Today's "global children" hold tomorrow's world in their hands!

Teach Me English & More English
Bind Up Edition
Book with CD
ISBN: 978-1-59972-608-3
Library of Congress Control Number: 2009901063

Copyright © 2009 Teach Me Tapes, Inc.
6016 Blue Circle Drive
Minnetonka, MN 55343-9104
www.teachmetapes.com
1-800-456-4656

Printed in the United States of America
10 9 8 7 6 5 4 3 2

Teach me...
ENGLISH

A Musical
Journey
Through
the Day

by
Judy Mahoney

A fun and unique way to introduce children to English as a second language

Teach Me...™
www.teachmetapes.com

 The More We Get Together

The more we get together, together, together,
The more we get together, the happier we'll be.
For your friends are my friends
And my friends are your friends
The more we get together, the happier we'll be.

Hello, my name is Marie.
What is your name?
This is my family.

My father

My mother

Me

My brother, Peter

My cat.

Her name is Fluffy.
She is soft and grey.

My dog.

His name is Spot.
He is black and white.

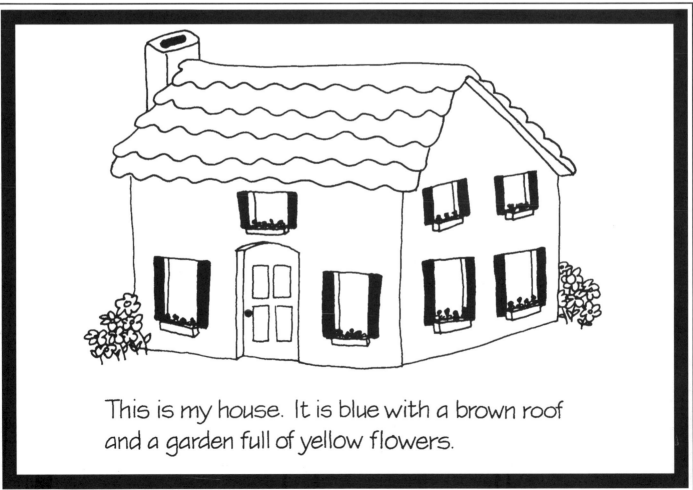

This is my house. It is blue with a brown roof
and a garden full of yellow flowers.

My room is red.
It's seven o'clock.
Get up! Get up!

 Are You Sleeping

Are you sleeping, are you sleeping?
Brother John, Brother John?
Morning bells are ringing
Morning bells are ringing
Ding, dang, dong! Ding, dang, dong!

 Lazy Marie

Lazy Marie, will you get up, will you get up, will you get up?
Lazy Marie, will you get up, will you get up today?
(Complete verses appear on page 16)

I get dressed.
I put on my shirt,

my pants,

my shoes,

and my hat.

For breakfast,
I like to eat cereal,
toast with jam and
drink orange juice.

head

shoulders

knees

toes

eyes

ears

mouth

nose

 Head, Shoulders, Knees and Toes

Head and shoulders, knees and toes, knees and toes.
Head and shoulders, knees and toes, knees and toes.
Eyes and ears and mouth and nose.
Head and shoulders, knees and toes, knees and toes.

Today is Monday! Do you know the days of the week?

MONDAY

TUESDAY

WEDNESDAY

THURSDAY

FRIDAY

SATURDAY

SUNDAY

Oh! It's raining! I wish the sun would come out.

Rain, Rain, Go Away
Rain, rain, go away,
Come again another day.
Rain, rain, go away,
Little Johnny wants to play.

It's Raining, It's Pouring
It's raining, it's pouring,
The old man is snoring,
He bumped his head and went to bed
And couldn't get up in the morning.

Rainbows
Sometimes blue and sometimes green
Prettiest colors I've ever seen
Pink and purple, yellow—whee!
I love to ride those rainbows.
© Teach Me Tapes, Inc. 1985

8 EIGHT

Here is my school.
Today I will repeat the numbers and alphabet.
Will you say them with me?

This Old Man

This old man, he played one;
He played knick-knack on my thumb.

Chorus:
With a knick-knack paddy whack,
Give a dog a bone;
This old man came rolling home.

This old man, he played two;
He played knick-knack on my shoe.
(Chorus)

This old man, he played three;
He played knick-knack on my knee.
(Chorus)

This old man, he played four;
He played knick-knack on my door.
(Chorus)
(Complete verses appear on page 17)

One Elephant

One elephant went out to play,
Upon a spider's web one day.
He had such enormous fun,
That he called for another elephant to come.

Two elephants went out to play,
Upon a spider's web one day.
They had such enormous fun,
That they called for another elephant to come.

Three ... (repeat)
Four ... (repeat)

All the elephants went out to play,
Upon a spider's web one day.
They had such enormous fun,
That they called for another elephant to come.

If You're Happy and You Know It

If you're happy and you know it,
Clap your hands. (clap, clap)
If you're happy and you know it,
Clap your hands. (clap, clap)
If you're happy and you know it,
Then your face will surely show it;
If you're happy and you know it,
Clap your hands. (clap, clap)

If you're angry and you know it,
Stomp your feet. (stomp, stomp)
If you're angry and you know it,
Stomp your feet. (stomp, stomp)
If you're angry and you know it,
Then your face will surely show it;
If you're angry and you know it,
Stomp your feet. (stomp, stomp)
(Complete verses appear on page 17)

The Puppets

Watch them hop, skip, jump,
Oh, the puppets they can go.
Watch them turn, fall, stand,
You must not miss the show.

Can we still come back,
To watch the puppets go.
Can we still come back,
Even when we are all grown.

After school,
we ride home in the car.

The Wheels on the Car

The wheels on the car go round and round,
Round and round, round and round,
The wheels on the car go round and round,
All around the town.

The horn on the car goes beep beep beep,
Beep beep beep, beep beep beep,
The horn on the car goes beep beep beep,
All around the town.

The wipers on the car go swish swish swish,
Swish swish swish, swish swish swish,
The wipers on the car go swish swish swish,
All around the town.

The lights on the car go blink blink blink,
Blink blink blink, blink blink blink,
The lights on the car go blink blink blink,
All around the town.

The driver of the car says, "Buckle up,"
"Buckle up, buckle up,"
The driver of the car says, "Buckle up,"
All around the town.

The children in the car say, "Let's have lunch,"
"Let's have lunch, let's have lunch,"
The children in the car say, "Let's have lunch,"
All around the town.

It is time for lunch. After lunch, I take a quiet time.

 Hush Little Baby

Hush little baby don't say a word,
Papa's gonna buy you a mockingbird;
If that mockingbird won't sing,
Papa's gonna buy you a diamond ring.
If that diamond ring turns brass,
Papa's gonna buy you a looking glass;
If that looking glass falls down,
You'll still be the sweetest little baby in town.

Hush little baby don't say a word,
Mama's gonna buy you a mockingbird;
If that mockingbird won't sing,
Mama's gonna buy you a diamond ring.
If that diamond ring turns brass,
Mama's gonna buy you a looking glass;
If that looking glass falls down,
You'll still be the sweetest little baby in town.

On the Bridge of Avignon

On the bridge of Avignon,
They're all dancing, they're all dancing.
On the bridge of Avignon,
They're all dancing round and round.

The Seasons Song

I like to rake the leaves
Into a big hump
Then I step back
Bend my knees, and jump!

I like to make a snowball
And roll it on the ground
It grows into a snowman
So big and fat and round.

©Teach Me Tapes, Inc. 1993
(Complete verses appear on page 18)

After my quiet time,
I go to the park to play.
I like to feed the ducks.
I sing and dance on the
bridge with my friends.

Six Little Ducks

Six little ducks that I once knew,
Fat ones, skinny ones, fair ones too.
But the one little duck
With the feather on his back,
He led the others with his
Quack, quack, quack...(repeat)
He led the others with his
Quack, quack, quack.
(Complete verses appear on page 19)

Our Mother Earth

Our Mother Earth
It's our home
It's the only one we have.

Our Mother Earth
It's our home
We need to keep it clean.

©Copyright Teach Me Tapes, Inc. 1993
(Complete verses appear on page 19)

I'm hungry! It must be time for dinner!

 Oh! Susanna

Well, I come from Alabama with a banjo on my knee,
I'm goin' to Louisiana, my true love for to see.
Oh, Susanna, oh, won't you cry for me.
'Cause I come from Alabama with a banjo on my knee.

It's night time. Do you see the stars? Good night, Mom. Good night, Dad. I love you!

Good night, my friends.

 Twinkle, Twinkle

Twinkle, twinkle, little star,
How I wonder what you are.
Up above the world so high,
Like a diamond in the sky,
Twinkle, twinkle, little star,
How I wonder what you are!

Lullaby

Lullaby and good night,
With roses delight.
Creep into your bed,
There pillow your head.
If God will, you shall wake,
When the morning does break.
If God will, you shall wake,
When the morning does break.
(Complete verses appear on page 19)

PAGE 1

The More We Get Together
The more we get together, together, together,
The more we get together, the happier we'll be.
For your friends are my friends
And my friends are your friends
The more we get together, the happier we'll be.

PAGE 2

Hello, my name is Marie. What is your name?
This is my family. My mother, my father,
my brother, Peter, and me.

PAGE 3

My cat. Her name is Fluffy. She is soft and grey.
My dog. His name is Spot. He is black and white.
This is my house. It is blue with a brown roof
and a garden full of yellow flowers.

PAGE 4

My room is red. It's seven o'clock.
Get up! Get up!

Are You Sleeping
Are you sleeping, are you sleeping?
Brother John, Brother John?
Morning bells are ringing
Morning bells are ringing
Ding, dang, dong! Ding, dang, dong!

Lazy Marie
Lazy Marie, will you get up, will you get up,
will you get up?
Lazy Marie, will you get up, will you get up
today?

Lazy Marie, will you get dressed, will you get
dressed, will you get dressed?
Lazy Marie, will you get dressed, will you get
dressed today?

Lazy Marie, please brush your teeth, brush your
teeth, brush your teeth.
Lazy Marie, please brush your teeth, please
brush your teeth today.

Lazy Marie, please wash your face, wash your
face, wash your face.
Lazy Marie, please wash your face, please wash
your face today.

Lazy Marie, please make your bed, make your
bed, make your bed.
Lazy Marie, please make your bed, please make
your bed today.

PAGE 5

I get dressed. I put on my shirt, my
pants, my shoes and my hat. For breakfast,
I like to eat cereal, toast with jam, and drink
orange juice.

PAGE 6

Head, Shoulders, Knees and Toes
Head and shoulders, knees and toes, knees
and toes.
Head and shoulders, knees and toes, knees
and toes.
Eyes and ears and mouth and nose.
Head and shoulders, knees and toes, knees
and toes.

PAGE 7

Today is Monday. Do you know the
days of the week? Monday, Tuesday,
Wednesday, Thursday, Friday,
Saturday, Sunday.

PAGE 8

Oh! It's raining! I wish the sun would come out!

Rain, Rain, Go Away
Rain, rain, go away,
Come again another day.
Rain, rain, go away,
Little Johnny wants to play.

It's Raining, It's Pouring
It's raining, it's pouring,
The old man is snoring,
He bumped his head and went to bed
And couldn't get up in the morning.

Rainbows
Sometimes blue and sometimes green
Prettiest colors I've ever seen
Pink and purple, yellow-whee!
I love to ride those rainbows.
© Teach Me Tapes, Inc. 1985

PAGE 9

Here is my school. Today, I will repeat the
numbers and alphabet. Will you say them with
me? One, two, three, four, five, six, seven, eight
nine, ten. Yeah!
A, B, C, D, E, F, G,
H, I, J, K, L, M, N, O, P,
Q, R, S, T, U, V,
W, X, Y and Z.
Now I know my ABCs, next time won't you sing
with me?

PAGE 10
This Old Man
This old man, he played one;
He played knick-knack on my thumb.

Chorus:
With a knick-knack paddy whack,
Give a dog a bone;
This old man came rolling home.

This old man, he played two;
He played knick-knack on my shoe.
(Chorus)

This old man, he played three;
He played knick-knack on my knee.
(Chorus)

This old man, he played four;
He played knick-knack on my door.
(Chorus)

This old man, he played five;
He played knick-knack on my hive.
(Chorus)

This old man, he played six;
He played knick-knack on my sticks.
(Chorus)

This old man, he played seven;
He played knick-knack up in heaven.
(Chorus)

This old man, he played eight;
He played knick-knack on my gate.
(Chorus)

This old man, he played nine;
He played knick-knack on my spine.
(Chorus)

This old man, he played ten;
He played knick-knack once again.
(Chorus)

One Elephant
One elephant went out to play,
Upon a spider's web one day.
He had such enormous fun,
That he called for another elephant to come.

Two elephants went out to play,

Upon a spider's web one day.
They had such enormous fun,
That they called for another elephant to come.

Three ... (repeat)
Four ... (repeat)

All the elephants went out to play,
Upon a spider's web one day.
They had such enormous fun,
That they called for another elephant to come.

If You're Happy and You Know It
If you're happy and you know it,
Clap your hands. (clap, clap)
If you're happy and you know it,
Clap your hands. (clap, clap)
If you're happy and you know it,
Then your face will surely show it;
If you're happy and you know it,
Clap your hands. (clap, clap)

If you're angry and you know it,
Stomp your feet. (stomp, stomp)
If you're angry and you know it,
Stomp your feet. (stomp, stomp)
If you're angry and you know it,
Then your face will surely show it;
If you're angry and you know it,
Stomp your feet. (stomp, stomp)

If you're silly and you know it,
Laugh out loud. (giggle)
If you're silly and you know it,
Laugh out loud. (giggle)
If you're silly and you know it,
Then your face will surely show it;
If you're silly and you know it,
Laugh out loud. (giggle)

If you're hungry and you know it,
Rub your tummy. (Mmm, Mmm)
If you're hungry and you know it,
Rub your tummy. (Mmm, Mmm)
If you're hungry and you know it,
Then your face will surely show it;
If you're hungry and you know it,
Rub your tummy. (Mmm, Mmm)

If you're sleepy and you know it,
Take a nap. (sigh)
If you're sleepy and you know it,
Take a nap. (sigh)

SONGS & DIALOGUE

If you're sleepy and you know it,
Then your face will surely show it;
If you're sleepy and you know it,
Take a nap. (sigh)
©Teach Me Tapes, Inc. 1993

The Puppets
Watch them hop, skip, jump,
Oh, the puppets they can go.
Watch them turn, fall, stand,
You must not miss the show.

Can we still come back,
To watch the puppets go.
Can we still come back,
Even when we are all grown.
©Teach Me Tapes, Inc. 1993

PAGE 11
After school, we ride home in the car.

The Wheels on the Car
The wheels on the car go round and round,
Round and round, round and round,
The wheels on the car go round and round,
All around the town.

The horn on the car goes beep beep beep,
Beep beep beep, beep beep beep,
The horn on the car goes beep beep beep,
All around the town.

The wipers on the car go swish swish swish,
Swish swish swish, swish swish swish,
The wipers on the car go swish swish swish,
All around the town.

The lights on the car go blink blink blink,
Blink blink blink, blink blink blink,
The lights on the car go blink blink blink,
All around the town.

The driver of the car says, "Buckle up,"
"Buckle up, buckle up,"
The driver of the car says, "Buckle up,"
All around the town.

The children in the car say, "Let's have lunch,"
"Let's have lunch, let's have lunch,"
The children in the car say, "Let's have lunch,"
All around the town.
©Teach Me Tapes, Inc. 1993

PAGE 12
Lunch Dialogue
Marie: "Hi, Mom! What's for lunch?"
Mom: "Would you like soup with peanut butter and jelly sandwiches?"
Marie: "Mmm, that sounds good. Chips, too?"
Mom: "Sure. What did you do in school today?"
Marie: "My teacher read us a story, I drew a picture, did some math, sang in music class and played baseball at recess."
Mom: "How nice. I'm happy you like school so much!"

It is time for lunch. After lunch, I take a quiet time.

Hush Little Baby
Hush little baby don't say a word,
Papa's gonna* buy you a mockingbird;
If that mockingbird won't sing,
Papa's gonna buy you a diamond ring.
If that diamond ring turns brass,
Papa's gonna buy you a looking glass;
If that looking glass falls down,
You'll still be the sweetest little baby in town.
(Repeat substituting "Mama" for "Papa")
*"gonna" is slang for "going to"

PAGE 13
After my quiet time, I go to the park to play. I like to feed the ducks. I sing and dance on the bridge with my friends.

On the Bridge of Avignon
On the bridge of Avignon,
They're all dancing, they're all dancing.
On the bridge of Avignon,
They're all dancing round and round.

The Seasons Song
I like to rake the leaves
Into a big hump
Then I step back
Bend my knees, and jump!

I like to make a snowball
And roll it on the ground
It grows into a snowman
So big and fat and round.

I am a little flower
My leaves are newly green

SONGS & DIALOGUE

When you see my first bud
You know it's spring; it's spring.

It is now summer
The sun is shining bright
Our days are all our own
To stand and fly a kite.

©Teach Me Tapes, Inc. 1993

Six Little Ducks

Six little ducks that I once knew,
Fat ones, skinny ones, fair ones too.
But the one little duck
With the feather on his back,
He led the others with his
Quack, quack, quack,
Quack, quack, quack,
Quack, quack, quack.
He led the others with his
Quack, quack, quack.

Down to the river they would go,
Wibble, wibble, wibble, wobble, all in a row.
But the one little duck
With the feather on his back,
He led the others with his
Quack, quack, quack.

Our Mother Earth

Our Mother Earth
It's our home
It's the only one we have.

Our Mother Earth
It's our home
We need to keep it clean.

The paper
The plastic
The glass should be recycled
It's you
It's me
Together we can save our Earth.

©Teach Me Tapes, Inc. 1993

PAGE 14
I'm hungry! It must be time for dinner.

Oh! Susanna

Well, I come from Alabama
With a banjo on my knee,
I'm goin' to Louisiana, my true love for to see.
Oh, Susanna, oh, won't you cry for me.

'Cause I come from Alabama
With a banjo on my knee.

PAGE 15
*It's night time. Do you see the stars? Good
night, Mom. Good night, Dad. I love you.*

Twinkle, Twinkle

Twinkle, twinkle, little star,
How I wonder what you are.
Up above the world so high,
Like a diamond in the sky,
Twinkle, twinkle, little star,
How I wonder what you are!

Lullaby

Lullaby and good night,
With roses delight.
Creep into your bed,
There pillow your head.
If God will, you shall wake,
When the morning does break.
If God will, you shall wake,
When the morning does break.

Lullaby and good night,
Those blue eyes closed tight.
Bright angels are near,
So sleep without fear.
They will guard you from harm,
With fair dreamland's sweet charm.
They will guard you from harm,
With fair dreamland's sweet charm.

Good Night, My Friends

Good night, my friends, good night
Good night, my friends, good night
Good night, my friends,
Good night, my friends,
Good night, my friends, good night

Good night!

Teach me more... ENGLISH

by
Judy Mahoney

A Musical Journey Through the Year

Learn English the fun way!

Teach Me...™
www.teachmetapes.com

MARIE: Hello. My name is Marie. This is my brother. His name is Peter. We have a dog. His name is Spot. We have a cat. Her name is Fluffy. Follow us through the year.

♪ **You'll Sing a Song**
You'll sing a song and I'll sing a song, and we'll sing a song together.
You'll sing a song and I'll sing a song, in warm or wintry weather.

Words and music by Ella Jenkins, ASCAP. Copyright 1966. Ell-Bern Publishing Co. Used by permission.

PETER: It is spring. I plant a flower garden. Look at my white and yellow daisies!

MARIE: I plant seeds to grow fruit and vegetables in my garden. This year, I will grow strawberries, tomatoes, carrots, cabbage and pumpkins.

Oats and Beans and Barley

Oats and beans and barley grow,
Oats and beans and barley grow.
Do you or I or anyone know
How oats and beans and barley grow?

(Complete verses appear on page 16)

White Coral Bells

White coral bells upon a slender stalk.
Lilies of the valley deck our garden walk.
Oh, don't you wish,
That you could hear them ring?
That can happen only when the fairies sing.

APRIL

Going to the Zoo

Momma's taking us to the zoo tomorrow,
Zoo tomorrow, zoo tomorrow
Momma's taking us to the zoo tomorrow,
We can stay all day.
Chorus:
We're going to the zoo, zoo, zoo
How about you, you, you?
You can come too, too, too
We're going to the zoo, zoo, zoo.

Look at all the monkeys swingin' in the trees...
Look at all the crocodiles swimmin' in the water...

MARIE: Today we will go to the zoo. Look at the lion, the giraffe and the monkey.

PETER: My favorite animal at the zoo is the crocodile.

Tingalayo

Tingalayo, come little donkey come.
Tingalayo, come little donkey come.
Me donkey fast, me donkey slow,
Me donkey come and me donkey go.
Me donkey fast, me donkey slow,
Me donkey come and me donkey go.

(Complete verses appear on page 16.)

MARIE: My birthday is May 10. I have a party with my friends.
My mother bakes me a big, round cake.
PETER: OK. Now it's time to play "Simon Says!"

Happy Birthday
Happy birthday to you!

"Simon Says"
Simon says: ... "put your right hand on your head."
... "touch the ground."
... "walk."
... "clap your hands."
... "say your name."
"Laugh out loud." "Simon didn't say!"

PETER: After spring, it is summer. In the summer, we go to the beach. I bring my beach ball and toy boat.

MARIE: I bring my sand pail and shovel to the beach.

PETER: We put on our swimsuits and build huge castles in the sand.

MARIE: Spot, don't knock it down!

Sailing, Sailing

Sailing, sailing,
Over the bounding main
For many a stormy wind shall blow
'Til Jack comes home again.

Row, Row, Row Your Boat

Row, row, row your boat
Gently down the stream
Merrily, merrily, merrily, merrily
Life is but a dream.

Down by the Seashore

Down by the seashore
Watch the little sea gulls
As they waddle down the beach
All in a row.

Down by the seashore
See the little tug boats
Pulling all the oil tankers
All in a row.

© Teach Me Tapes, Inc. 1994

(Complete verses appear on page 17)

MARIE: After we swim, we eat our picnic lunch. We eat peanut butter sandwiches, cheese, carrots and bananas. It is delicious!
PETER: Oh no! Look at the ants!
MARIE: After our picnic, we go for a walk.

The Things of the Ocean

Little drops of water
Little grains of sand
Make the mighty ocean
So beautiful and grand.

Little bubbles floating
Little snails that slide
Make the mighty ocean
So beautiful and grand.

Every fish and coral
Every bird and clam
Make the mighty ocean
So beautiful and grand.

Every weed and turtle
Every whale and crab
Make the mighty ocean
So beautiful and grand.

Gentle dolphins swimming
Gentle rolling waves
Make the mighty ocean
So beautiful and grand.

Gentle gliding pelicans
A gentle seal at rest
Make the mighty ocean
So beautiful and grand.

(Complete verses appear on page 17)

MARIE: Today, we go to the natural history museum.
PETER: It is my favorite place because there are so many
dinosaurs. Look at the triceratops. It has three horns on its head.

MARIE: Next, we go across the street to visit the art musuem.
PETER: I like to look at the bulls in Goya's painting. I pretend I am the matador.
MARIE: Look at the painting by Van Gogh. The flowers in his painting look like the ones in my garden.

Brown Girl in the Ring

Brown girl in the ring,
Tra-la-la-la-la (repeat)
She looks like a sugar
And a plum, plum, plum!

2. Show me a motion ...
3. Skip across the ocean ...
4. Do the locomotion ...

MARIE: After summer, it is autumn. The leaves turn gold, red and orange. We gather leaves and acorns that fall from the trees.

The Green Grass Grew

There was a tree
In all the woods,
The prettiest tree
That you ever did see.

The tree in the hole
And the hole in the ground,
The green grass grew all around, all around
And the green grass grew all around.

And on that tree ...
There was a limb ...

And on that limb ...
There was a branch ...

And on that branch ...
There was a twig ...

And on that twig ...
There was an acorn ...

(Complete verses appear on page 18)

PETER: Before we go back to school, we visit Grandpa's farm. We feed the cows, chickens and pigs.

MARIE: Grandpa shears the wool from the sheep. Later, he takes us on a hayride with our cousins.

Baa Baa Black Sheep

Baa baa black sheep, have you any wool?
Yes sir, yes sir, three bags full.
One for my master and
One for my dame,
One for the little boy
Who lives down the lane.
Baa baa black sheep, have you any wool?
Yes sir, yes sir, three bags full.

Down on Grandpa's Farm

Oh, we're on our way, we're on our way
On our way to Grandpa's farm. (repeat)

Down on Grandpa's farm there is a big brown cow (repeat)
The cow, she makes a sound like this: Moo! (repeat)

... there is a little red hen (repeat)
The hen, she makes a sound like this: Cluck! Cluck! (repeat)

Old MacDonald

Old MacDonald had a farm, E I E I O
And on that farm he had a cow, E I E I O
With a moo, moo here,
And a moo, moo there
Here a moo, there a moo,
Everywhere a moo, moo
Old MacDonald had a farm, E I E I O

... had a chicken, cat, some sheep.

MARIE: Today, our parents take us to the fall festival. We bring the vegetables from our garden to be judged.
PETER: There are many rides for the children. I love to ride the merry-go-round.

PETER: It is Halloween. I am carving a face on my pumpkin.
MARIE: Tonight, I will dress up in my Little Red Riding Hood costume and Spot will be the wolf. Peter will be a cowboy. Then we will go trick or treating with our friends.
PETER: After Halloween, it is November.

Five Little Pumpkins

Five little pumpkins sitting on a gate
First one said, "Oh my, it's getting late."
Second one said, "There are witches in the air."
Third one said, "But we don't care."
The fourth one said, "Let's run and run and run."
The fifth one said, "I'm ready for some fun."
"Oo-oo," went the wind, and out went the light,
And the five little pumpkins rolled out of sight.

PETER: Look, snow is falling. Let's go and play in the snow. We take our sleds and slide down the hill.

MARIE: Then we'll build a huge snowman. He has coal eyes, a carrot nose and a derby hat. He wears my mother's scarf.

Snowman Song

There's a friend of mine
You might know him, too
He wears a derby hat
He's real cool.

He has coal black eyes
An orange carrot nose
Two funny stick-like arms
And a snowy overcoat.

Have you guessed his name
Or do you need a clue?
You'll never see his face
In autumn, summer, spring.

©Teach Me Tapes, Inc. 1989

Silent Night

Silent night, holy night,
All is calm, all is bright.
'Round yon Virgin, Mother and child
Holy infant, so tender and mild,
Sleep in heavenly peace,
Sleep in heavenly peace.

MARIE: It is holiday time. We celebrate Christmas. We bake cookies and decorate our house. We sing special songs.

PETER: January first begins the new year. We have a party to celebrate on New Year's Eve.

America the Beautiful

Oh, beautiful for spacious skies.
For amber waves of grain.
For purple mountains majesty,
Above the fruited plain.

America, America,
God shed His grace on thee.
And crown thy good with brotherhood,
From sea to shining sea.

MARIE: In February, we celebrate the Mardi Gras carnival. It is fun. I like to catch candy at the parade. We wear costumes and sing and dance with our friends.

PETER: Now we know the months of the year. Do you? January, February, March, April, May, June, July, August, September, October, November, December. Good-bye!

SONGS & DIALOGUE

PAGE 1
You'll Sing a Song
You'll sing a song and I'll sing a song,
And we'll sing a song together.
You'll sing a song and I'll sing a song,
In warm or wintry weather.

Words and music by Ella Jenkins. ASCAP
Copyright 1966. Ell-Bern Publishing Co. Used by permission.

MARIE: Hello. My name is Marie. This is my brother. His name is Peter. We have a dog. His name is Spot. We have a cat. Her name is Fluffy. Follow us through the year.

PAGE 2 MARCH
PETER: It is spring. I plant a flower garden. Look at my white and yellow daisies!
MARIE: I plant seeds to grow fruit and vegetables in my garden. This year, I will grow strawberries, tomatoes, carrots, cabbage and pumpkins.

Oats and Beans and Barley
Oats and beans and barley grow,
Oats and beans and barley grow.
Do you or I or anyone know
How oats and beans and barley grow?

First the farmer plants the seeds,
Stands up tall and takes his ease,
Stamps his feet and claps his hands
And turns around to view his land.

Then the farmer waters the ground,
Watches the sun shine all around,
Stamps his feet and claps his hands
And turns around to view his land.

White Coral Bells
White coral bells upon a slender stalk.
Lilies of the valley deck our garden walk.
Oh, don't you wish, that you could hear them ring?
That can happen only when the fairies sing.

PAGE 3 APRIL
MARIE: Today we will go to the zoo. Look at the lion, the giraffe and the monkey.
PETER: My favorite animal at the zoo is the crocodile.

Going to the Zoo
Momma's (Daddy's) taking us to the zoo tomorrow,
Zoo tomorrow, zoo tomorrow
Momma's (Daddy's) taking us to the zoo tomorrow,
We can stay all day.
Chorus:
We're going to the zoo, zoo, zoo
How about you, you, you?
You can come too, too, too
We're going to the zoo, zoo, zoo.

2. Look at all the monkeys swingin'* in the trees...
3. Look at all the crocodiles swimmin'** in the water...

Words & music by Tom Paxton. Copyright 1961, renewed 1989.
Cherry Lane Music Publishing Co., Inc.
All rights reserved. Used by permission.

*"swingin'" is slang for "swinging"
**"swimmin'" is slang for "swimming"

Tingalayo
Tingalayo, come little donkey come.
Tingalayo, come little donkey come.
Me donkey fast, me*** donkey slow,
Me donkey come and me donkey go.
Me donkey fast, me donkey slow,
Me donkey come and me donkey go.

Tingalayo, come little donkey come.
Tingalayo, come little donkey come.
Me donkey he, me donkey haw,
Me donkey sleep in a bed of straw.
Me donkey dance, me donkey sing,
Me donkey wearing a diamond ring.

***"Me" is slang for "my."

PAGE 4 MAY
Happy Birthday to You
Happy birthday to you!

MARIE: My birthday is May 10. I have a party with my friends. My mother bakes me a big, round cake.
PETER: OK. Now it's time to play "Simon Says!"

Simon Says Game
Simon says: ... "put your right hand on your head."
                 ... "touch the ground."
                 ... "walk."
                 ... "clap your hands."
                 ... "say your name."
                     "Marie, Peter, Jenny, Joey."
"Laugh out loud." "Simon didn't say!"

PAGE 5 JUNE
PETER: After spring, it is summer. In the summer, we go to the beach. I bring my beach ball and toy boat.
MARIE: I bring my sand pail and shovel to the beach.
PETER: We put on our swimsuits and build huge castles in the sand.
MARIE: Spot, don't knock it down!

Row, Row, Row Your Boat
Row, row, row your boat
Gently down the stream.
Merrily, merrily, merrily, merrily
Life is but a dream.

Sailing, Sailing
Sailing, sailing, over the bounding main
For many a stormy wind shall blow
'Til Jack comes home again.

Down by the Seashore
Down by the seashore
Watch the little sea gulls
As they waddle down the beach
All in a row.

Down by the seashore
See the little tug boats
Pulling all the oil tankers
All in a row.

Down by the seashore
See the little sailboats
As they glide across the waves
All in a row.

Down by the seashore
See the little girls
As they build their sand castles
All in a row.

Down by the seashore
See the little boys
As they race their toy boats
All in a row.

Down by the seashore
See the sun is setting
Watch the people as they leave
All in a row.
©Teach Me Tapes, Inc. 1994

PAGE 6 JULY
MARIE: After we swim, we eat our picnic lunch. We eat peanut butter sandwiches, cheese, carrots and bananas. It is delicious!
PETER: Oh no! Look at the ants!
MARIE: After our picnic, we go for a walk.

The Things of the Ocean
Little drops of water
Little grains of sand
Make the mighty ocean
So beautiful and grand.

Little bubbles floating
Little snails that slide
Make the mighty ocean
So beautiful and grand.

Every fish and coral
Every bird and clam
Make the mighty ocean
So beautiful and grand.

Every weed and turtle
Every whale and crab
Make the mighty ocean
So beautiful and grand.

Gentle dolphins swimming
Gentle rolling waves
Make the mighty ocean
So beautiful and grand.

Gentle gliding pelicans
A gentle seal at rest
Make the mighty ocean
So beautiful and grand.

All the tiny sea shells
All the tiny bugs
Make the mighty ocean
So beautiful and grand.

All the tiny treasures
On the tiny islands
Make the mighty ocean
So beautiful and grand.
©Teach Me Tapes, Inc. 1994

PAGE 7 AUGUST
MARIE Today, we go to the natural history museum.
PETER: It is my favorite place because there are so many dinosaurs. Look at the triceratops. It has three horns on its head.

PAGE 8 AUGUST
MARIE: Next, we go across the street to visit the art museum.
PETER: I like to look at the bulls in Goya's painting. I pretend I am the matador.
MARIE: Look at the painting by Van Gogh. The flowers in his painting look like the ones in my garden.

Brown Girl in the Ring
Brown girl in the ring,
Tra-la-la-la-la (repeat)
She looks like a sugar
And a plum, plum, plum!

2. Show me a motion...
3. Skip across the ocean...
4. Do the locomotion...

PAGE 9 SEPTEMBER
MARIE: After summer, it is autumn. The leaves turn gold, red and orange. We gather leaves and acorns that fall from the trees.

The Green Grass Grew
There was a tree
In all the woods,
The prettiest tree
That you ever did see.

The tree in the hole
And the hole in the ground,
The green grass grew all around, all around
And the green grass grew all around.

And on that tree ...
There was a limb ...

And on that limb ...
There was a branch ...

And on that branch ...
There was a twig ...

And on that twig ...
There was an acorn ...

And by that acorn ...
There was a leaf ...

The leaf by the acorn
And the acorn on the twig
And the twig on the branch
And the branch on the limb
And the limb on the tree
And the tree in the hole
And the hole in the ground,
The green grass grew all around, all around
And the green grass grew all around.

PAGE 10 OCTOBER
PETER: *Before we go back to school, we visit Grandpa's farm. We feed the cows, chickens and pigs.*
MARIE: *Grandpa shears the wool from the sheep. Later, he takes us on a hayride with our cousins.*

Down on Grandpa's Farm
Oh, we're on our way, we're on our way
On our way to Grandpa's farm. (repeat)
Down on Grandpa's farm there is a big brown cow (repeat)
The cow, she makes a sound like this: Moo! (repeat)

... there is a little red hen (repeat)
    The hen, she makes a sound like this: Cluck! Cluck! (repeat)

Baa Baa Black Sheep
Baa baa black sheep, have you any wool?
Yes sir, yes sir, three bags full.
One for my master and
One for my dame,
One for the little boy who lives down the lane.
Baa baa black sheep, have you any wool?
Yes sir, yes sir, three bags full.

Old MacDonald
Old MacDonald had a farm, E I E I O
And on that farm he had a cow, E I E I O
With a moo, moo here and a moo, moo there
Here a moo, there a moo, everywhere a moo, moo
Old Mac Donald had a farm, E I E I O.

... had a chicken, cat, some sheep.

PAGE 11 OCTOBER
MARIE: *Today our parents take us to the fall festival. We bring the vegetables from our garden to be judged.*
PETER: *There are many rides for the children. I love to ride the merry-go-round.*

PAGE 12 OCTOBER AND NOVEMBER
PETER: *It is Halloween. I am carving a face on my pumpkin.*
MARIE: *Tonight, I will dress up in my Little Red Riding Hood costume and Spot will be the wolf. Peter will be a cowboy. Then we will go trick or treating with our friends.*
PETER: *After Halloween, it is November.*

Five Little Pumpkins
Five little pumpkins sitting on a gate
First one said, "Oh my, it's getting late."
Second one said, "There are witches in the air."
Third one said, "But we don't care."
The fourth one said, "Let's run and run and run."
The fifth one said, "I'm ready for some fun."
"Oo-oo," went the wind, and out went the light,
And the five little pumpkins rolled out of sight.

PAGE 13 DECEMBER
PETER: *Look, snow is falling. Let's go and play in the snow. We take our sleds and slide down the hill.*
MARIE: *Then we'll build a huge snowman. He has coal eyes, a carrot nose and a derby hat. He wears my mother's scarf.*

Snowman Song
There's a friend of mine
You might know him, too
He wears a derby hat
He's real cool.

He has coal black eyes
An orange carrot nose
Two funny stick-like arms
And a snowy overcoat.

Have you guessed his name
Or do you need a clue?
You'll never see his face
In autumn, summer, spring.

Who is it?
Can you guess?
C'mon, guess!
C'mon, don't you know?
It's the snowman!
©Teach Me Tapes, Inc. 1989

Silent Night
Silent night, holy night,
All is clam, all is bright.
'Round yon Virgin, Mother and Child,
Holy infant so tender and mild,
Sleep in heavenly peace,
Sleep in heavenly peace.

PAGE 14 DECEMBER AND JANUARY
*MARIE: It is holiday time. We celebrate Christmas.
We bake cookies and decorate our house. We sing
special songs.*
*PETER: January first begins the new year. We have a
party to celebrate on Hew Year's Eve.*

America the Beautiful
Oh, beautiful for spacious skies.
For amber waves of grain.
For purple mountains majesty,
Above the fruited plain.
America, America,
God shed his grace on thee.
And crown thy good with brotherhood,
from sea to shining sea.

PAGE 15 FEBRUARY
*MARIE: In February, we celebrate the Mardi Gras
carnival. It is fun. I like to catch candy at the parade.
We wear costumes and sing and dance with our
friends.*
*PETER: Now we know the months of the year. Do
you?*

*January, February, March, April, May, June, July,
August, September, October, November, December.*

Good-bye!

NOTES

NOTES

Spring Vocabulary
Label the picture with the following words

soil	garden
strawberries	tulip
vegetables	carrots
pumpkin	flowers
cabbage	sunflower
tomato	sun

SUMMER

Summer Vocabulary
Label the picture with the following words

clouds	cup
lake	thermos
beach	sunglasses
ant	swimsuit
sand	cheese
blanket	shoes
banana	shirt
sailboat	sandwich

AUTUMN

Autumn Vocabulary
Label the picture with the following words

sky	bird
leaves	dog
sweater	jacket
cat	basket
skirt	pants
nut	tree

WINTER

Winter Vocabulary
Label the picture with the following words

hill	ice skates
jacket	snow
ice	scarf
snowflake	eye
sled	carrot
hat	stick
coat	mitten
snowman	mouth

A B C D E F G H I J K L M N O P Q R S T U V W X Y Z

Alphabet

A  ant	B  balloon	C  car	D  dinosaur	E  eyes
F  flowers	G  guitar	H  horn	I  insect	J  jacket
K  Koala	L  lion	M  marionettes	N  nose	O  owl
P  pail	Q  queen	R  rainbow	S  sun	T  table
U  umbrella	V  violin	W  whale	X  xylophone	Y  yarn	Z  zebra